CONFESSIONS
OF A **WOLF CRYER**

From Little Boy to Mature Man

CHRIS WHEEL, SR.

Copyright © 2024 Chris Wheel, Sr.

ISBN: 979-8-9913067-0-6

All rights reserved.

No part of this publication may be reproduced, distributed, or transmitted in any form or by any means, including photocopying, recording, or other electronic or mechanical methods, without the prior written permission of the publisher, except as permitted by U.S. copyright law.

Printed in the United States of America.

As a recovering wolf cryer, I'm thankful for the community I've been blessed to have in my life throughout my journey from boyhood to manhood. Many people have played a vital role in my maturation, and I am beyond thankful. There are too many to name, and for that, I am blessed. However, I would be remiss if I didn't thank my Lord and Savior Jesus for the gift of life, learning, loving, and leading. It is a blessing to experience these gifts through the support of my wife, Gina; my kids, Jasmine, Kezia, Jaimena, Briana, and Chris Jr.; my mom, Cynthia; my siblings; and so many more. Without your love, patience, correction, and prayers, none of this would have been possible. Thank you, and I look forward to many more opportunities to brag about my community.

ACKNOWLEDGMENTS

There's always a fear of singling out people when providing acknowledgments, as it's inevitable that someone might be overlooked. So many people have played a part in shaping me and motivating me to finish this project, whether they knew it or not. Please blame any omissions on my head, not my heart. If I missed mentioning you, let it serve as motivation for me to write many more books to ensure everyone gets a shout-out of love and admiration.

I have to start by thanking my amazing wife,

Gina. From the start of our marriage, you've been supportive and patient as I've shared my heart and passions. You gave me space when needed and pushed me when needed to complete this project and others. There were times I wanted to quit, but you didn't let me, and I'm forever grateful.

I want to thank the best mom ever, Cynthia Wheel. You are the OC, the original cheerleader from the beginning of my journey. You've been that steady presence and giver of unconditional love through my ups and downs. Although Dad is not with us now, the two of you have been instrumental in shaping me into a man that doesn't cry wolf anymore but has stepped up to the challenge of being part of the change and not the problem we see in our society today. Thank you, and I love you.

I could go on and on about the tremendous impact you have had in my life, sis. Dr. Karen Wheel-Carter, you are and continue to be my "shero." From the time I was a little boy to now, you have always challenged me to not accept mediocrity but to strive for greater things. You saw in me something that I didn't see in myself and not only told me but showed me how to draw it out. You've led by example and left a path for me to follow and continue to achieve. Thank you, big sis! I love you.

I'm thankful for you, James Loftis, for your friendship and support over the years. We've laughed hard, served hard, encouraged hard, cried hard, and prayed hard. We've seen many fathers and father figures go through our fatherhood program. It's been a blessing having your support and heart to help men become better fathers. Somewhere in that process, we've seen God manifest in our parenting the lessons we've shared with so many. Thank you for your belief in me and encouragement to create a resource for the countless fathers we've served and new fathers we will serve in the future.

I want to thank you, Dena Crecy, for your support and encouragement for me to complete the book projects I've been telling you about for years. Your friendship and model of what it looks like to pursue your dreams and not give up have been what I needed. Seeing you finish several book projects while pouring out to others in many ways has been an inspiration and conviction. Thank you for not letting me make any excuses and providing me with the resources I needed to get this particular book project completed. I thank you and truly appreciate you beyond words.

I'm thankful to Callie Revell for your professional support and guidance through this project. Although it was my first of many books, you have made this process pleasant, fun, and exciting. Your willingness to be patient with me has truly been a major blessing and helped me to enjoy this journey. Thank you again.

I want to thank all the men and women that make up The Turn•Around Agenda Team. Your thoughts, prayers, encouragement, and interest in this project have been a great motivator for me to continue and finish the work. I'm looking forward to more projects that I can share as well as enjoying the projects you will complete as well. Let's keep encouraging one another to do great things. Thank you.

I want to thank Dr. Evans and the OCBF Family. I came a broken young man, and over the years, through the grace of God, the powerful messages, prayers, worship, fellowship, and opportunity to serve, I've matured. I'm not perfect, but I'm confident that I serve a perfect God who loves me perfectly. Your continued prayers and encouragement are always needed and truly a blessing. Thank you.

Lastly, I want to thank the thousands of fathers and father figures in the community that I've had the privilege and opportunity to serve and encourage. This book encompasses some of those same principles I've shared with you, and I'm thankful to have had some small influence in your lives. It is my hope that this book will be a resource for you to use as needed to continue your development and engagement with your family and friends. You matter, and I'm thankful for you.

CONTENTS

"IT IS EASIER TO BUILD STRONG CHILDREN THAN TO REPAIR BROKEN MEN."

—FREDERICK DOUGLASS

INTRODUCTION

Have you ever heard of the story of "The Little Boy Who Cried Wolf"? I heard this story as a little boy, and it captivated me. It helped me formulate a viewpoint that I held long into my adult years and have passed on to my kids.

Some of you may already know what I'm about to say. We've always been taught that the moral of the story is not to cry wolf.

Over the years, I've dwelled on this story as an adult. It led me to make a deep, introspective evaluation of the story—even the moral I've held so dearly about not lying. It wasn't until I was asked to speak at a fatherhood event at a local school that I unlocked a deeper perspective about the little boy, the wolf, the villagers, and the sheep. What was once a little kid's story now became the basis for an important talk that I would like to spend some time sharing with you.

I'm not sure if you've heard about this book through someone else, or maybe you've even heard me speak somewhere. Perhaps the title of this book stood out to you and you decided to give it a read. Whatever the reason, I'm thankful you are here. I believe the insights and lessons in this book will resonate with your own personal journey, helping you more deeply engage with your family, friends, and community. I hope you will find your investment of time in reading this book worthwhile.

Unlike the original story we heard as kids, this book is tailored toward men of all ages. As we delve deeper into this wonderful short story, I hope you will agree that the lessons and insights are more expansive and impactful than you could ever imagine. They can profoundly influence how you engage with those around you. So, let's not delay any longer. Let's take a stroll down Memory Lane, or for some, a drive down Discovery Boulevard.

Chapter 1

THE STORY

There once was a little boy who was asked to watch the sheep. As he watched, he became bored and decided to play a trick on the villagers. He cried, "Wolf!" and as he predicted, they rushed to his aid, only to discover they had been tricked. They scolded him and told him not to cry wolf unless there was a real threat.

Since the little boy had tricked them once, he decided to do it again. To the villagers' surprise and anger, there again wasn't a wolf, and the little boy had a good laugh about it. The villagers repri-

manded him and went back to the village, leaving the little boy there alone to watch the sheep. For a while, he sat there and contemplated whether he should do it again. He decided he would, despite the two previous warnings.

As he got ready to cry wolf, a real wolf came out of the woods and attacked the sheep. Frantically, the little boy cried, "WOLF!" as loud as he could over and over. But no one came to his defense. Sadly, the wolf was able to kill several sheep before retreating back into the woods. Devastated, the little boy ran to the village to break the news of what happened. He and the village were saddened by the great loss.

For those of you familiar with it, what were you taught was the moral of the story? Let us all together say, "You shouldn't cry wolf." To cry wolf is to lie. Wow. No matter how many times I tell this story at meetings, workshops, Bible studies, or other events, everyone always agrees that the moral is *you shouldn't cry wolf*. I used to believe that too, until something happened.

Periodically, I'm invited to speak at fatherhood events. One time in particular, I was preparing my speech to share. I needed a good opening that the

fathers, father figures, and their children could relate to since it would be a mixed crowd of children
and adults. I asked myself the question, *What can
all of them relate to from their childhood?* Perhaps a
nursery rhyme or children's story wouldn't take
long to explain.

I tried different ones until I remembered "The
Little Boy Who Cried Wolf." I liked that story, and
it had a good message. So, I started to rehearse it
with the rest of my speech and realized that something was wrong. As an adult revisiting that story,
a horrible reality started to form in my mind versus
what I remembered as a kid. Viewing the story
through the lens of fatherhood, I immediately realized that all this time we were blaming the
wrong person for what happened to the sheep.
Why were we blaming a little boy?

And that's when it hit me right between my
eyes. Why was a little boy sent to do a man's job?
Why was a little boy left alone with the responsibility of watching the sheep? The more I thought
about the story, the more upset I became with the
villagers who failed to do the right thing—three
times. The first time was when they sent him to
watch the sheep. The second time was when they

realized he was being irresponsible, and they reprimanded him but left him with the sheep again. The third time was when they saw that he was being rebellious but reprimanded him again and still left him responsible for the sheep. What's the saying? "Fool me once, shame on you. Fool me twice, shame on me." Well, what do you say when it's three times? "Fool me three times, and the fool is me."

So, as you can imagine, I had a dilemma about my presentation and what I would say to those attending the fatherhood event. I literally wrestled with this revelation of the little boy, and I wanted to exonerate him and clear his name. I wanted to let all those families know that the real moral was little boys shouldn't be asked or expected to take on the responsibility of grown men. As I thought about it more and more, I realized that I was on to something, and I decided to share it with them. As you can imagine, it was well received and blew the minds of many of the men who were in attendance. It was so obvious, but we all missed it. We chose to embrace what we were taught as children and never took the time to revisit it as adults. We never learned the real takeaway for us as men.

My goal as we explore the next several chapters is to take you on a journey through this amazing story and uncover some of the hidden gems—underlying messages that are as relevant to us today as they were so long ago.

SUMMARY

This chapter recounts the classic tale of "The Boy Who Cried Wolf," highlighting the boy's deceptive actions, the villagers' responses, and the eventual tragedy when a real wolf appears.

KEY TAKEAWAYS

- The boy's actions were driven by a need for attention and a lack of understanding of the consequences.

- The villagers failed to see the deeper issue and left the boy in a position of responsibility he was not ready for.

PRINCIPLES TO APPLY

- Always consider the underlying reasons behind actions, especially in children.

- Ensure that responsibilities are assigned to those who are mature and capable.

REFLECTIVE QUESTIONS

Have you ever dismissed someone's actions without understanding the root cause? What was the outcome?

_____

_____

_____

_____

_____

_____

_____

_____

_____

_____

_____

_____

_____

How do you determine if someone is ready for a specific responsibility?

_____

_____

_____

_____

_____

_____

_____

_____

_____

_____

_____

_____

_____

_____

What steps can you take to mentor someone who might be struggling with their responsibilities?

_____

_____

_____

_____

_____

_____

_____

_____

_____

_____

_____

_____

_____

_____

Chapter 2

THE CHARACTERS

I f you were to produce a play of this story, you would need to identify the characters. The main character is the little boy, the "protagonist." Supporting characters include the villagers, the sheep, and the wolf—the "antagonist." To understand these characters better, we will use a five-point approach: Initial State, Development, Crisis, Resolution, and Growth. Think of yourself as a detective solving a case, starting with the initial clues, developing theories, encountering a crisis, finding a resolution, and ultimately growing in your detective skills. Here's a mnemonic to re-member these points: "Ingenious Detectives Crack Really Great cases."

Let's start with the little boy and discuss his character development. Initially, he is bored and seeking attention, lacking a deeper understanding of the consequences of his actions. This is evident because he cried wolf three times—twice as a joke on the villagers and the last time for real. He knew a wolf was a threat and that the villagers would re-spond quickly, indicating he had been instructed on what to do if he ever encountered a wolf. De-spite this, he used this knowledge to play on the villagers' emotions, tapping into their deepest fears and concerns.

Wow! Either this boy was a manipulative ge-nius or simply a child seeking attention. Does this seem familiar? It should if you have kids. Even as babies, children can get our attention through cry-ing, complaining, begging, or lying—yes, lying. Over time, they learn more ways to get reactions. We see this in pets as well. If your dog needs to use the bathroom or wants attention, they will do cer-tain things to get the desired outcome.

As adults, we often continue to manipulate situations to our advantage, some better than others. Think of salespeople trained to get a response or scammers targeting vulnerable individuals. They play on the emotions of those they want to manipulate. Our moral character can sometimes be manipulative and immature. Immature boys can grow up to be immature men, irresponsible and negatively impacting others around them. Perhaps the men in the village wanted to do something different and tried letting the little boy watch the sheep. Maybe they were preoccupied with sports, women, alcohol, or other hobbies instead of mentoring the boy to ensure he was mature enough for the responsibility. Whatever the reason for their lack of foresight, entrusting a boy with a man's responsibility had significant consequences for the entire community.

Some of you may be wondering why this matters. I understand, and I want to make this point clear. The little boy had learned how to manipulate people long before he cried wolf, which made it easy for him to play such a serious joke despite the danger around him. His actions demonstrated his immaturity and failure to understand the responsibility he held. That's why it's curious they would send an immature boy to do a job meant for a mature man.

Notice I said mature man because it's possible to be an immature man in actions and attitude. Either someone chose to ignore the boy's character flaws or wasn't close enough to see his immaturity. They failed to mentor him and determine if he was ready for the responsibilities of being a good shepherd.

Initially, we see the men in the village hearing the cry of wolf and rushing together to address the perceived threat, but they failed to see the real threat underneath. When they thought a wolf was about to attack the sheep and potentially the little boy, they rushed to his aid. They were quick to respond to a perceived crisis instead of seeking a deeper solution.

Addressing a crisis doesn't require a relational connection. I don't have to like or know a person to help them if there is perceived danger. I may have a sense of concern and desire to assist, but that doesn't mean I will hang out afterward and get to know the person I helped. The goal is to help in the moment, not to establish an ongoing relationship. Men like to help, fix things, and find solutions to problems. That's a transactional relationship that only requires a temporary investment of time and aid.

However, a transformational relationship requires a long-term investment of emotions, commitment, time, vulnerability, and access. It's an ongoing engagement with someone before, during, and after a problem. The goal is a real long-term solution, not a temporary fix. This approach focuses on deeper-rooted issues rather than surface-level ones. It requires a mature man to look beyond his own interests and focus on developing and mentoring those who may be immature and still little boys in their attitude and actions.

The little boy might not have been so quick to cry wolf to manipulate the villagers if he had been mentored by a mature man from the village. It's important to understand this point: all of us are prone to make poor decisions if we don't have accountability, mentoring, and awareness of the expectations and risks of the responsibilities given to us. None of us are exempt from acting like the little boy if we've never had or don't currently have a mature man in our life holding us accountable, mentoring us to be the best versions of ourselves, and helping us see how to take our responsibilities seriously. We need to have access to their private and public lives. I can't stress this enough. If we are going to help little boys become mature men, we need to have transformational relationships rather than transactional ones. We need to recognize that the real threat is not the wolf, but the immature person who cries wolf.

So, have we cracked the case of why the wolf was able to cause so much pain and destruction yet? Remember our mnemonic, "Ingenious Detectives Crack Really Great cases"? We have discovered some initial clues about the character of the little boy and the villagers, and we've developed some theories on how a lack of personal growth and relational development contributed to the tragedy. But we must take a deeper look at the crisis that led to the devastating outcome before we can find a true resolution.

SUMMARY

This chapter analyzes the main characters in the story: the little boy, the villagers, the sheep, and the wolf, using a five-point approach: Initial State, Development, Crisis, Resolution, and Growth.

KEY TAKEAWAYS

- The little boy's immaturity and need for attention led to his irresponsible actions.
- The villagers' failure to mentor and guide the boy resulted in a lack of accountability and responsibility.

PRINCIPLES TO APPLY

- Develop transformational relationships rather than transactional ones.
- Focus on mentoring and guiding the next generation to ensure they are ready for their responsibilities.

REFLECTIVE QUESTIONS

Who are the key characters in your life, and how do they influence you?

_____

_____

_____

_____

_____

_____

_____

_____

_____

_____

_____

_____

Are your relationships primarily transactional or transformational? How can you shift towards transformational relationships?

_____

_____

_____

_____

_____

_____

_____

_____

_____

_____

_____

_____

_____

How can you actively mentor and guide someone in your community or family?

_____

_____

_____

_____

_____

_____

_____

_____

_____

_____

_____

_____

_____

_____

Chapter 3

THE INTERNAL CRISIS: THE BOY

In the last chapter, we developed some theories about how a lack of personal growth and relational development contributed to the tragedy in the village. As we delve deeper into these theories, it becomes clear that the story had both internal and external crises. Understanding the internal crisis will help us better understand the external one. If we simplify the resolution to "lying leads to tragedy," we miss the deeper issues that started long before the events of that day. We will focus on the symptoms rather than the root cause. Let's first examine the internal crisis, and then in the next chapter, we will explore the external crisis.

Long before the events of that day, the little boy was misled into believing life was a game to be played or to get played. This mindset made it easy for him to repeatedly play practical jokes on the villagers. He didn't value his life, and therefore, he didn't value others' lives either. This lack of value led him to shirk the serious responsibility of shepherding the sheep, turning it into a joke even when faced with the real danger of a wolf. He thought integrity, correction, accountability, and truth were optional. This is why he easily lied on two occasions, ignored the villagers' warnings, and still expected them to believe him when a real wolf appeared, endangering him and the sheep. Additionally, he felt his worth and value was tied to how people felt about him when he did a "service" they asked him to do, which left him feeling undervalued when not performing any service. That's why he was bored and lonely watching the sheep but did it to please the men who were only attentive when there was a perceived crisis.

Can you see how the little boy experienced an internal crisis? It might seem like an overreach, but the proof is in his behavior. His actions were rooted in a deeper conflict. He didn't come up with the idea to play that trick out of nowhere. Consider this: he had one job—to watch the sheep and alert the villagers if there was a wolf. The wolf posed a serious danger that couldn't be ignored, prompting the villagers to rush to action when they heard the cry of wolf. Comparing the wolf's threat with the boy's casual and irresponsible treatment of that threat as a joke reveals an internal crisis manifesting externally. Perhaps he felt undervalued and believed the only way to gain attention was through deception. Imagine a student who feels ignored by their teacher and acts out in class to get noticed. The boy's actions were similar, stemming from a deeper sense of being undervalued and misunderstood.

SUMMARY

This chapter delves into the internal crisis faced by the little boy, examining his beliefs and actions that led to the tragedy.

KEY TAKEAWAYS

- The boy's actions were a result of feeling undervalued and misunderstood.

- His lack of respect for others' lives and responsibilities led to serious consequences.

PRINCIPLES TO APPLY

- Address underlying emotional and psychological issues to prevent irresponsible behavior.

- Recognize and nurture the value in each individual to foster a sense of responsibility and respect.

REFLECTIVE QUESTIONS

Can you identify a time when you felt undervalued? How did it affect your behavior?

_____

_____

_____

_____

_____

_____

_____

_____

_____

_____

_____

_____

_____

_____

How do you show respect for others' responsibilities and lives in your daily interactions?

_____

_____

_____

_____

_____

_____

_____

_____

_____

_____

_____

_____

_____

What can you do to help someone who might feel undervalued or misunderstood?

_____

_____

_____

_____

_____

_____

_____

_____

_____

_____

_____

_____

_____

Chapter 4

THE INTERNAL CRISIS: THE VILLAGERS

This internal crisis wasn't limited to the little boy; the villagers, especially the men, faced several internal struggles. The first was a crisis of identity. They seemed to have forgotten their responsibilities to the village, the sheep, and especially the little boy. They placed him in a position for which he lacked experience, understanding, and capacity. They chose to relinquish their leadership to someone they should have been guiding. They were supposed to be the providers, protectors, and leaders of their families and community.

Whether due to the pressures of life, the weight of responsibilities, or the burnout of leadership, they chose to remain in the village while the little boy was left to do a man's job.

Another internal struggle the men in the village faced was the crisis of selfishness. Their self-interest didn't allow space or time to invest in the little boy. The boy most likely wasn't the only one in the village without the presence of a man willing to mentor him. He represented all the boys who lacked a male figure to guide and coach them on responsibility, emotional management, and the impact of their choices on others. In today's context, this can be likened to communities where one out of three fathers are absent from the home due to various reasons, leaving young boys without role models. Without mentorship, these boys might turn to negative influences like gangs and organized crime, mirroring the selfishness and lack of guidance seen in the village.

The lack of involvement from the village men created a vacuum of morals, values, and wisdom that the boy filled with his own flawed view of responsibility. These men missed an opportunity to show the boy how to protect, provide, and lead through shepherding. By selfishly choosing to leave the boy to manage on his own, they set the stage for a tragedy that would likely scar his mind, reputation, and confidence in being the best version of himself for years to come. He would have to live with the trauma of knowing his immaturity negatively impacted the lives of the sheep, the trust of the community, and his confidence in managing responsibilities.

In today's context, it's not unusual to see men with broken relationships, unproductive lives, and substance abuse issues due to childhood trauma. These men were once little boys with a future full of countless possibilities, but their choices and the choices of those around them have left a trail of hurt, confusion, and squandered opportunities.

Some may argue the boy deserved the fallout of "Wolfgate," but that's too easy. Why was he called out for his selfishness when he was only modeling what he saw from the men in the village? Three times they had the opportunity to guide him, but they chose to leave him alone. They left him to demonstrate his irresponsibility and try to figure out leadership on his own, literally leaving him to the wolves. After the second time the boy fooled them, they consciously decided not to return, even if they heard the cry of wolf. Sadly, they allowed a child's behavior to impede their duty to protect the sheep, the boy, and the village. They allowed his immaturity to become their irresponsibility. Their selfishness prevented them from recognizing that the boy was too immature to handle such responsibility without proper guidance and mentoring.

Lastly, they had an internal crisis of accountability. Why didn't someone stop for a moment and say, "This isn't a good idea," before they had him go watch the sheep? Considering what the sheep represented, this was obviously an important responsibility meant for someone mature, capable, and accountable. If they initially thought he was ready to do the job, why didn't they reconsider after the first and second times?

Because they lacked accountability. The sheep weren't just disposable pets or decorations. The sheep provided wool for clothing, blankets, and other necessary items for the village to thrive and sell or trade for their economy. The sheep provided meat and dairy for food and drink, sustaining the village. The sheep also benefited agriculture by grazing to maintain the landscape, and their manure could be used as fertilizer for gardens and crops. These aspects created economic stability by diversifying income sources, creating jobs, and establishing a cultural identity for generations. If the sheep represented all of that, why leave them in the hands of a boy who had repeatedly shown he wasn't responsible enough to do a man's job? It was a lack of accountability that ultimately led to a breakdown in the community—a breakdown in the economy, trust, security, confidence, jobs, and more. Again I ask, where was the accountability? The men had an internal crisis of accountability.

SUMMARY

This chapter explores the internal crises faced by the villagers, particularly the men, focusing on identity, selfishness, and accountability.

KEY TAKEAWAYS

- The villagers forgot their responsibilities and placed them on the boy, leading to a breakdown in accountability.

- Their selfishness and lack of involvement created a vacuum that the boy filled with his own flawed understanding.

PRINCIPLES TO APPLY

- Embrace and fulfill your roles and responsibilities to set a positive example.

- Invest time and effort in mentoring and guiding the younger generation.

REFLECTIVE QUESTIONS

Have you ever shirked a responsibility that should have been yours? What was the impact?

_____

_____

_____

_____

_____

_____

_____

_____

_____

_____

_____

_____

_____

In what ways can you show more involvement and guidance in your community or family?

_____

_____

_____

_____

_____

_____

_____

_____

_____

_____

_____

_____

_____

How do you ensure that you are accountable for your actions and decisions?

Chapter 5

THE EXTERNAL CRISIS

Having examined the profound internal crises facing the boy and villagers, we must now shift our attention to the inescapable external consequences of those unresolved issues. These unaddressed internal flaws precipitated a devastating public crisis on the day the wolf appeared. This external crisis was on full display for the entire village to see, negatively impacting everyone. As we look at some examples of this external crisis, we have to remember that what was happening on the inside influenced what was experienced on the outside. If we simplify the external crisis as merely a boy lying, leading to sheep being killed, we miss the bigger picture of the unfolding crisis. Let's take a look at some examples to better understand exactly what was going on.

The first example of the external crisis was the absence of men in roles of responsibility. This was evident when they put the little boy into a major position of responsibility and expected him to be accountable. Where were the men? We see them show up when they heard the cry of the wolf. Whether it was an adrenaline rush, the prompting of others in the village, the desire to not look scared, or to be a team player, they responded to the boy's cry of wolf and rushed to his aid. On the surface, this looks commendable. It looks like they were responsive, attentive, and caring. But looks can be deceiving.

I'm not saying that they didn't care about a wolf killing the sheep or the boy. I'm simply pointing out that they didn't show up until a little boy alerted them of perceived danger. Don't miss this point. They were responding to the leadership of a little boy instead of leading him. They weren't present to be the ones crying wolf. They were somewhere else, not where they should have been. They weren't present. Imagine all the little kids watching the men do whatever they were doing while a little boy was being the man of the community, the man of the house, the man of the family. Future generations were learning that it was okay to not be present and put your responsibilities off on those who should first be taught how to be responsible. They weren't present to lead because they were too busy reacting to problems between their other "priorities" instead of focusing on their main responsibility.

The second example of an external crisis was the crisis of public accountability, which should have served as a lesson for others to learn from bad decisions and improve themselves. This was evident when they didn't appropriately address the little boy who lied, rebelled, and created a public scare. As we mentioned earlier, the responsibility he had was too great for him to handle alone. When he demonstrated his immaturity and lack of regard for the public crisis he created, they should have publicly held him accountable to restore public confidence in the systems and leaders in place to protect, provide, and lead the community. This would have required the men to publicly undo the damage by taking their proper place to watch the sheep while mentoring the boy. This would have created a model for what men in the community should do for their kids—publicly demonstrating how to lead themselves, their families, and their community. This model would help stabilize the present while creating generational stability.

The last example of the external crisis was the crisis of the wolf. While the lack of leadership among the men presented an insidious internal threat, the wolf embodied a violent external force that could disrupt and destroy the village's way of life. A cunning predator, it saw the breakdown in accountability as an opportunity to exploit, mercilessly attacking the vulnerable sheep. The wolf exposed the weaknesses and challenges within the leadership in the community. It highlighted the selfishness of the men in the village and how easily trust could be broken, leading to tragedy. The community understood the threat of the wolf and was scared, but not scared enough to guard against it effectively. They sent a little boy to do a man's job.

Perhaps the wolf exposed how their comfortable economy led them to reprioritize what was important, focusing on their own cares over those of the community, the little boy, and the sheep. They became numb to the dangers of the wolf and essentially threw the boy to the wolves by sending him into a situation he was not equipped to handle. The wolf waited for the right opportunity to strike when there was a total breakdown in accountability, communication, trust, security, and integrity. The wolf knew the right time to attack when there was no threat to its plans to eat the sheep. It was cunning, strategic, stealthy, and relentless—traits not to be ignored or discarded. Alone, the little boy and the sheep were no match for the wolf. Even with the boy crying wolf, there wasn't enough time to stop the wolf from making off with at least one of the sheep.

How often had the villagers minimized the threat of the wolf? How many times did the wolf scout the scene to see if a man was anywhere to be found? How many times did the wolf see the boy and think, "Why isn't a man there with him?" How many times did the wolf plan to come back for more? The wolf was a relentless and constant threat to much more than just the sheep. Why didn't they respect the impact of a wolf left unchecked?

The external crisis in that village had a profound impact that would reverberate for generations. Lives were lost and lives were altered for generations to come. Sadly, the little boy would never be the same. The village would never be the same. But hopefully, the men wouldn't be the same either and would make a change for the better. Because one thing is for certain: the wolf would never change. It would always be a threat as long as it lived, waiting for the right opportunity to steal, kill, and destroy. The only thing that would be a threat to it would be men who stopped living from crisis to crisis and sought resolutions to grow and become the providers, protectors, and leaders they were meant to be.

SUMMARY

This chapter examines the external crisis that resulted from the unresolved internal issues of the
boy and villagers, culminating in the wolf's attack.

KEY TAKEAWAYS

- The absence of responsible men in leadership roles led to the tragedy.
- Public accountability and proper guidance
  were lacking, exacerbating the crisis.

PRINCIPLES TO APPLY

- Be present and actively lead in your community and family.
- Hold individuals accountable in a constructive manner to foster growth and responsibility.

REFLECTIVE QUESTIONS

How can you be more present and active in your community or family?

What steps can you take to ensure accountability in your personal and professional life?

_____

_____

_____

_____

_____

_____

_____

_____

_____

_____

_____

_____

_____

How do you respond to crises, and what can you do to improve your approach to leadership and guidance?

_____

_____

_____

_____

_____

_____

_____

_____

_____

_____

_____

_____

_____

Chapter 6

A RESOLUTION FOR GROWTH

T here's a saying that nothing changes if nothing changes. This is true in every aspect of life. If nothing different happens than what has already happened, then whatever happens will keep happening. I know that sounds like a tongue twister, but it's a crucial point that we need to examine for better understanding. Another way of looking at this is the definition of insanity: doing the same thing over and over again and expecting different results. If we are going to have a growth resolution, we must understand the purpose. We must understand the why. Without a vision for what change looks like, we risk experiencing more tragedy, trauma, and trials.

Remember our mnemonic, "Ingenious Detectives Crack Really Great cases?" Are you ready to crack the case of Wolfgate? Well, let's review our notes. We know what happened: the boy was asked to watch the sheep. We know the boy twice tricked the villagers into believing there was a wolf when there wasn't one. We know they had scolded him for playing tricks on them. We know the little boy cried wolf for the villagers to come and rescue the sheep from the wolf. We know the villagers didn't come and later found out that the little boy really saw a wolf that time. We know a wolf attacked and killed the sheep for food. All of these are facts that we know. However, we are trying to discover the truth. We have the facts, but we need the truth about why the tragedy occurred and how it can be prevented from happening again. In our investigation, we learned about the character of the little boy, the villagers, and even the wolf. We really didn't spend much time talking about the sheep. We also discussed theories on how a lack of personal growth and relational development led to the crisis experienced in the village, both internally and externally. Now, we are ready to look at all the evidence we've gathered to crack the case and develop a resolution for growth and change.

As mentioned earlier, we must have a "why," a purpose for changing and growing. After the tragedy, the villagers and the little boy had to do some soul searching. They had to decide how they would live their lives moving forward. Some might revert to their old ways, but others would never want to experience that pain and loss again. They recognized the need for change to ensure the wolf wouldn't exploit their vulnerabilities and kill more sheep.

The little boy faced three considerations for growth. First, he needed to understand his value and the value of the villagers and sheep. His lack of respect led to a breakdown in trust and communication, allowing the wolf to access the sheep unhindered. We can see this played out in families today when marriages fall apart because of communication and trust issues, leading to the children being caught in the middle, emotionally scarred and taken advantage of by predators because of their need for affection.

Second, he had to grasp that his choices, good or bad, had significant consequences. He learned the hard way that a joke can lead to major, unintended outcomes. An example of this in today's context are teenagers creating dangerous challenges on social media for likes and attention that often have deadly consequences, prompting public outrage and calls for change. The little boy, too, needed to change his attitude and behavior to avoid being a liability to the village and the sheep. If he continued his behavior, the village would have to restrict his responsibilities and opportunities.

Lastly, he needed to embrace coaching and correction. The boy had rejected accountability and correction before the loss of the sheep, leading to the villagers' cold shoulder due to his lying. He required accountability, coaching, mentoring, and intervention. If he accepted these changes, healing could occur, fostering trust, respect, and forgiveness throughout the village. A phrase sometimes used in counseling circles is, "If you can feel it, then you can heal it."

Like the little boy, the men in the village had to own up to their areas for growth and change. They needed to acknowledge their shortcomings and how these allowed the wolf to get the sheep. The men had vital roles to play for the village's protection and progress. They had three main areas to focus on. First, they were providers, bringing back resources necessary for the village's survival and betterment, including food, trade items, or raw materials. Second, they needed to protect the village from outside threats like the wolf, other predators, and people with selfish motives, as well as natural or man-made disasters. But there were also inside threats.

These inside threats could be similar to some of the outside threats but also very different. For example, internal divisions and strife could lead to conflict and potential escalation, threatening the village's stability. Another inside threat was the spread of disease, which needed to be identified and isolated for the village's well-being. If too many villagers were sick, it could leave the village vulnerable. However, one often overlooked inside threat had a generational impact and long-term implications for the community's sustainability. This inside threat was at the heart of the problem that led to Wolfgate.

This last threat highlights the third role and area of focus for the men in the village: accountability and mentoring for the young boys. This inside threat was hard to see because it came with blinders passed down through generations. It didn't start overnight and wasn't initially widespread. It was a slow-growing issue that could eventually undermine the village if not addressed. The little boy needed a mentor, a coach, a father figure to guide him to maturity. Perhaps there was a father, but his absence led to the tragic event. Even if the father wasn't around, other men should have stepped up to ensure the boy wasn't alone.

This issue wasn't isolated; their willingness to send a boy to do a man's job revealed a deeper problem. Their apathy in allowing the boy to stay despite his immaturity shows they either didn't know how to lead or didn't care. For change and growth, the men needed to develop young men ready for responsibility. This required mentoring the boys. The inside threat was boys left to figure out how to be men. As long as the men were selfish and focused on themselves, they modeled this behavior to the boys. Sadly, these boys would grow up looking out for their own self-interests. This inside threat led to an outside tragedy, but if the men matured and made a real change, they could be the providers, protectors, and father figures needed to guide the next generation and help the village thrive.

We've focused a lot on the men in the village, and rightfully so. However, women and young girls were also essential for the village's growth. They played a vital role in ensuring that day-to-day tasks were met and contributed significantly to the economy by processing and developing resources and goods. Yet, they couldn't do their part effectively if the men weren't fulfilling their responsibilities. It took the collective efforts of all to help the village thrive. That's why their voices were important. Like the men, the women should have spoken up about the boy's immaturity. The boy's mother, in particular, should have seen that he wasn't ready for such a responsibility. Although she might have tried or ignored the signs, after the first incident, she could have insisted on changing who watched the sheep. We may never know her role in the decision, but she would have been a key voice in vouching for or against his character. For positive change to occur, the women needed to speak up more or be listened to more. Their involvement in their boys' lives was crucial.

The final piece of the puzzle, or the last clue to develop a growth resolution, is the sheep. While they might seem like innocent victims, they were a significant part of the tragedy and are crucial to the growth resolution.

To better understand the tragedy as it pertains to the sheep, we must recognize their dependency on the shepherd. As mentioned earlier, the sheep needed to be protected from various external and internal threats. Sheep, for the most part, are animals that depend on someone else to provide for and protect them. If the sheep have a good shepherd, they will thrive and have many productive years. Several external threats could compromise these productive years, such as predators looking to devour them. Sheep are not able to put up a fight against predators or other animals that can injure them, like snakes and even insects like flies. When sheep are sheared, there is the fear of infection or bugs eating at the area and causing further issues. They are basically sitting targets that can't outrun or outfight predators. Additionally, sheep are in danger of environmental threats like drowning in water because of their wool. Another external danger is Mother Nature. Again, sheep aren't able to guard against adverse weather conditions, nor can they source their own food. They have to be led to areas that are sustainable for their diet. The last external threat is them getting isolated, lost, or stuck in areas where their wool gets caught and they can't get loose. These external factors are important to understand because the shepherd's responsibility was to be watchful and attentive against these threats.

Some of the internal threats are infections and parasites, which could create major health challenges and possible death for the sheep. The shepherd would need to attend to those wounds and potential infections in various ways. Another internal threat is the sheep's lack of intelligence. Sometimes sheep are called stupid or not bright. Their ability to get out of their own way is lacking and can create a lot of work for the shepherd. When dealing with many sheep, this can be a daunting task. That's why it was a dangerous thing to put unintelligent sheep with an immature boy. At some point, trouble was going to occur. The real issue was what the fallout would be. Unfortunately for them, in this case, it ended in tragedy.

Now, let's focus on the growth resolution for the sheep. The sheep provided essential resources for the village: wool for textiles, milk for drink or food, and meat for sustenance. They could also be bred for long-term provision or traded for additional supplies and resources. The sheep were a significant investment and a large part of the village's economy. Without them, the village would suffer or depend on other villages for sustainability. Creating an environment where sheep can flourish involves minimizing threats and risks. This requires a strategic plan to combat threats and ensure only mature individuals shepherd the sheep. The reality of this responsibility should drive future behavior, ensuring the sheep are safe. If the men step up and lead, they should watch the sheep while training others to take on this responsibility. The sheep, loyal to their shepherd, need consistent leadership. It's crucial not to let the wrong voices influence the sheep. They require a consistent presence for long-term productivity.

For the men to take their role as shepherds seriously, they needed to step up and create an environment where the sheep could prosper by minimizing threats and risks. This required admitting their wrongs and making them right. They had to mature and become the providers, protectors, and father figures needed to nurture and guide the next generation.

SUMMARY

This chapter discusses the steps needed for growth and change, focusing on the boy, the villagers, and the sheep.

KEY TAKEAWAYS

- Understanding one's value and the impact of choices is crucial for personal growth.

- Embracing accountability, coaching, and mentoring can lead to healing and improvement.

PRINCIPLES TO APPLY

- Seek and provide mentorship to foster maturity and responsibility.

- Develop a strategic plan to address threats and ensure a safe and productive environment.

REFLECTIVE QUESTIONS

How do you perceive your own value, and how does it influence your choices?

_____

_____

_____

_____

_____

_____

_____

_____

_____

_____

_____

_____

_____

In what areas of your life could you benefit from mentorship or coaching?

_____

_____

_____

_____

_____

_____

_____

_____

_____

_____

_____

_____

_____

What steps can you take to create a strategic plan for personal growth and community improvement?

_____

_____

_____

_____

_____

_____

_____

_____

_____

_____

_____

_____

Chapter 7

THE CONCLUSION

Congratulations! You've cracked the case of Wolfgate. You've discovered the problem and the resolution. Although this story about a little boy has been shared with kids around the world, its message extends far beyond the ears of the next generation. Its relevance is more expansive than we could have ever imagined. Think about your own life and ask: *How am I helping or hurting those around me? Who is dependent on me, and how am I managing that relationship? What are some things I need to address in my life, and in what ways can I mature? What potential threats do I need to be mindful of, and what adjustments should I make for myself and my sphere of influence?*

While we may not always know when the wolf will come to steal, kill, and destroy, we can prepare ourselves to handle the threats. We must also nurture and develop the next generation to ensure our communities thrive long after we are gone. Each of us has a voice, and we can't be afraid to speak up and hold each other accountable. We need to look beyond our self-interest and focus on improving the lives of those around us. This requires discipline, accountability, and understanding the worth and value of ourselves and others. We can make the world a better place, one family at a time, one community at a time, if we stop sending little boys to do a mature man's job. The choice is yours. Choose wisely, and when you hear the cry of wolf, you'll be ready.

SUMMARY

The final chapter ties together the themes and lessons from the previous chapters, encouraging readers to reflect on their own lives and actions.

KEY TAKEAWAYS

- The story's message extends beyond the next generation, emphasizing the importance of personal growth and community responsibility.
- Each individual has the power to make a positive impact by fulfilling their roles and responsibilities.

PRINCIPLES TO APPLY

- Continuously develop yourself to handle life's challenges effectively.
- Nurture and guide the next generation to ensure the long-term success and well-being of your community.

REFLECTIVE QUESTIONS

How are you currently contributing to the well-being of your community and family?

_____

_____

_____

_____

_____

_____

_____

_____

_____

_____

_____

_____

_____

What areas of personal growth do you need to focus on to better handle life's challenges?

_____

_____

_____

_____

_____

_____

_____

_____

_____

_____

_____

_____

_____

How can you nurture and guide the next generation to ensure their success and well-being?

_____

_____

_____

_____

_____

_____

_____

_____

_____

_____

_____

_____

_____

APPENDIX

PRACTICAL TIPS AND ACTIONABLE STEPS TO SUCCESS

PERSONAL DEVELOPMENT

Practical Tips:

1. **Self-Reflection:** Regularly take time to reflect on your values, beliefs, and actions. Use journaling or meditation to gain insights into your personal growth. Refer to Chapter 3 to understand the importance of self-awareness in personal development.

2. **Set Goals:** Define clear, achievable goals for your personal and professional life. Break

them down into smaller, manageable tasks. This mirrors the strategic planning discussed in Chapter 6.

3. **Continuous Learning:** Commit to lifelong learning. Read books, take courses, and seek out new experiences. The boy's growth in the story underscores the necessity of ongoing education and self-improvement.

REFLECTION

ACTIVE INVOLVEMENT

Practical Tips:

1. **Community Participation:** Get involved in your local community through volunteering, attending town meetings, or participating in local events. Chapter 4 highlights the impact of active involvement in creating a thriving community.

2. **Family Engagement:** Spend quality time with your family. Engage in activities that strengthen bonds and foster open communication. The story's emphasis on family dynamics can guide this effort.

3. **Be Present:** Show up for others, both in good times and in crises. Be a dependable presence in your relationships. Chapter 5 illustrates the consequences of neglecting this principle.

REFLECTION

Confessions of a Wolf Cryer

_____

_____

_____

_____

_____

_____

_____

_____

_____

_____

_____

_____

_____

_____

_____

_____

ACCOUNTABILITY

Practical Tips:

1. **Accountability Partners:** Establish relationships with individuals who can hold you accountable for your actions and goals. This concept is explored in Chapter 4.

2. **Transparent Communication:** Be open and honest in your communications. Address mistakes promptly and take responsibility for your actions, as advised in Chapter 5.

3. **Regular Check-Ins:** Schedule regular check-ins with your accountability partners to review progress and address any challenges.

REFLECTION

_____

_____

_____

_____

_____

_____

Confessions of a Wolf Cryer

_____

_____

_____

_____

_____

_____

_____

_____

_____

_____

_____

_____

_____

_____

_____

_____

MENTORING

Practical Tips:

1. **Identify Mentees:** Look for opportunities to mentor others, particularly those younger or less experienced. The boy's need for mentoring in the story is a key lesson from Chapter 4.

2. **Be a Role Model:** Demonstrate the behaviors and values you wish to instill in your mentees. Lead by example, as discussed in Chapter 2.

3. **Offer Support and Guidance:** Provide ongoing support, guidance, and constructive feedback. Help your mentees navigate challenges and celebrate their successes.

REFLECTION

_____

_____

_____

_____

LEADERSHIP

Practical Tips:

1. **Lead with Integrity:** Ensure your actions align with your values and principles. Integrity is a cornerstone of effective leadership, as highlighted throughout this book.

2. **Empower Others:** Encourage and empower those around you to take on responsibilities and develop their skills. This mirrors the transformational leadership approach discussed in Chapter 6.

3. **Vision and Strategy:** Develop a clear vision and strategy for your team or organization. Communicate this vision effectively and involve others in achieving common goals.

REFLECTION

_____

_____

_____

_____

ABOUT THE AUTHOR

Rev. Christopher "Chris" Wheel stands as a cornerstone at Oak Cliff Bible Fellowship in Dallas, Texas, fulfilling two pivotal roles that define his extensive ministry and community outreach work.

As the Associate Pastor of Outreach, Chris is deeply devoted to fostering global community impact. His tireless dedication ensures that the church's outreach initiatives not only align with the teachings of Jesus but also create lasting ripples of positive change on a worldwide scale. Chris's leadership in this area is marked by a commitment to embodying God's purpose through action, ensuring that every program and initiative serves the community in diverse and meaningful ways. He passionately pursues the church's mission: "To Disciple the Church to Impact the World." This mission shapes his work by guiding his efforts to disciple believers, enabling them to make a significant impact on their communities and beyond.

In his role as the Executive Director of the Turn·Around Agenda, Chris guides and oversees four main areas of social outreach:

- Public School Outreach
- Family Services
- TECS Program (Technology, Education, and Career Services)
- Resale Store

Each facet of this agenda is meticulously designed to serve the community, addressing various needs and empowering individuals through practical support and spiritual guidance. The mission of the Turn·Around Agenda is to transform communities by developing leaders and strengthening families. Through these programs, Chris ensures that the ministry provides opportunities and training to engage the community, the country, and the world, living out the mission to Disciple the Church to Impact the World. His leadership ensures these programs are effective in transforming lives and strengthening communities.

One of the cornerstone programs under Chris's leadership is the Public School Outreach. This initiative engages students through mentoring and coaching, providing guidance and support to help them navigate their educational journey and personal development. Additionally, the program extends its reach to parents, offering basic needs assistance and programs designed to help them achieve a turnaround in their lives, thus strengthening the family unit. Over the past 16 years, Chris has also focused on working with fathers through fatherhood classes, certified through the National Fatherhood Initiative. He has mentored fathers in prisons, courts, community classes, and public schools, launching numerous fatherhood programs, Dad's Clubs, and more. These efforts are aimed at empowering fathers to play a more active and positive role in their families and communities.

Chris's journey is marked by over 25 years of multifaceted professional experience. He has served in roles ranging from an elementary school teacher and a corporate trainer to a global training manager. In 1996, as a chaplain assistant in the U.S. Army, Chris deployed to Kuwait with the 1st Cavalry Division, 8th Engineer Battalion from Fort Hood, Texas. During this time, he learned the true meaning of selfless sacrifice, the importance of supporting others, the power of a "we first" mindset, and the necessity of being mission-focused. These experiences profoundly shaped his approach to ministry and leadership.

Educationally enriched, Chris holds a Bachelor's degree in English Education from Old Dominion University and a Master's in Biblical Counseling from Dallas Theological Seminary. His educational journey has also been marked by a strong focus on leadership, personal, and professional development. This continuous learning has equipped him with the tools necessary to mentor and guide others effectively. He is also a certified pre-marital and marital consultant through Prepare and Enrich, helping couples build strong, healthy relationships.

Beyond his duties at Oak Cliff Bible Fellowship, Chris is deeply intertwined with the national non-profit fabric. He serves on various boards, lending his expertise to multiple ministries and organizations within the DFW area. His involvement extends his impact, allowing him to contribute to broader community efforts and initiatives, always with the goal of making a lasting difference in line with his mission-driven work.

Chris's extensive experience in corporate

training and coaching has allowed him to help organizations with professional development, strategic planning, and team collaboration. His ability to lead and inspire has made a significant impact on the organizations and individuals he has worked with, fostering growth and development in various professional settings.

Central to Chris's world is his family. He is a devoted husband to Gina and a father to five children—four daughters and one son. As a proud grandfather, his commitment to family and service shines brightly in every endeavor, embodying the principles of leadership and strength that he champions in his professional life.

Rev. Chris Wheel's life is a testament to the power of faith, dedication, and service. His journey, marked by significant contributions and unwavering commitment, continues to inspire and impact countless lives, embodying the true essence of living out God's purpose. Through his work, he not only fulfills his roles with excellence but also consistently aligns his efforts with the overarching missions that guide and shape his path.

Made in the USA
Middletown, DE
02 September 2024

60267414R00066